ESSENTIAL QUESTIONS

FOR

EDUCATORS

GUIDING YOUR GROWTH AS A TEACHER
THROUGH QUESTIONS THAT MATTER

ESSENTIAL QUESTIONS

FOR

EDUCATORS

BILL BROOKS

Published by
EQ4E Press

ISBN:
979-8-9953760-0-2 (paperback)
979-8-9953760-1-9 (hardcover)
979-8-9953760-2-6 (eBook)

Cover and interior design by Ian Koviak
Edited by Lisa Juliano

Printed in the United States of America

For Dani

and all the other educators who show up for their students daily.

A piece of my life, offered honestly.

BILL BROOKS

CONTENTS

PART 1

FINDING YOUR FOOTING
QUESTIONS, LEARNING, AND THE WORK OF BECOMING

BEFORE WE BEGIN

What you're about to read isn't meant to be a system. It isn't a framework, and it isn't even an answer.

It's a collection of questions I've learned to carry.

They're the ones that have changed how I show up in rooms, how I listen to people, and how I design learning – not because they're complete, but because they refuse to let things go numb.

I don't believe there is an alpha and omega of teaching – no final form, no moment where you arrive and stay.

There is only this unfinished work of paying attention again:

to students,
to colleagues,
to yourself.

The questions in this book aren't meant to point you toward a perfect way to teach.

They're meant to keep you awake inside the work – helping you notice when something feels alive in a lesson, pause when something isn't quite working, and keep asking.

If this book does anything useful, I hope it's this:

that it nudges you toward the questions that feel most alive in your work – the ones that follow you into lessons, conversations, and long drives home.

Teaching doesn't end when a workshop finishes. It doesn't end when a strategy stops feeling new, and it definitely doesn't end when someone closes a book.

The bells keep ringing.

Students keep arriving.

And the real work continues.

These pages are an invitation –

to stay in the work,
to keep choosing how you show up,
and to remember that growth – real growth – almost never announces itself.

It asks you to continue.

And if questions really do keep us awake inside the work,

then it makes sense to start with one that sits at the center of everything we do.

1 WHEN A QUESTION FINDS YOU

Kathy was retiring.

Her room was already half-packed, the kind of half-packed that feels heavier than full. Posters were coming down. Desk drawers were emptied. A whole career was being quietly folded into cardboard boxes. Midmorning light slanted across the room, catching the edges of stacked papers and leaving long shadows over the student desks.

I was her assistant principal at the time – technically her evaluator – but that day none of that mattered much. She had spent years in that room. I had walked in near the end of that story, and part of me recognized that I was sitting in the presence of something I didn't yet fully understand.

"I still can't believe you're retiring," I said.

"Me neither," she smiled. "But I know it's time."

I sat down in one of the student desks. The room felt different without kids in it – quieter, lighter. As if it were holding its breath.

"So… what was it all for?" I asked. "What's the point of all this?"

She didn't hesitate.

"I want students to learn," she said. "And I want them to think for themselves."

That sounded right. It still sounds right.

But even then, it didn't feel finished.

"How do we make that happen?" I asked. "Is there more to it than just learning and thinking?"

We talked for a long time after that – about curiosity, frustration, and the kids who surprised us. About the lessons that fell flat and the ones that somehow caught fire. About the strange mixture of intention and mystery that lives inside teaching.

Somewhere in that conversation, without trying to, we started circling a question. I didn't know it yet, but it would follow me out of that room and into almost everything that came next.

I didn't find that question in a framework or a book. I stumbled into it that morning in Kathy's classroom, and once it arrived, it didn't leave. It followed me into classrooms, into post-observation conferences, into moments when I wasn't proud of how I had shown up – and into moments when I was.

Over time it became a kind of mirror – not a checklist, not a goal, but a way of noticing.

When I think back on my own teaching – and later on my work alongside other teachers – I can trace almost everything I care about back to that moment.

Not because the question gives me answers.

Because it keeps asking something of me.

It asks something when I'm frustrated.
It asks something when I'm hopeful.
It asks something when I realize I've been going through
the motions.

And sometimes it sits there in silence, just as it did in Kathy's empty
room, waiting for me to notice what I'm doing and why.

This book grows out of that question and everything it stirred in me.
Not because I've figured it out – but because I haven't.

I keep circling the same tension:

How much of learning lives in what we teach,
and how much lives in how we show up?

How much of a classroom does the curriculum build,
and how much do the small, human moments that never make it into
lesson plans contribute?

I don't have clean answers to those questions. I only know they keep
shaping the way I see students, lessons, and myself.

Maybe they'll start doing that for you too.

The question born in Kathy's empty classroom?

How will I behave with my students and design my lessons to
increase the probability students will learn, wonder about, and have
passion for my content?

Pause and Reflect

Pause for a moment with the question that grew out of this chapter.

Essential Question

How will I behave with my students and design my lessons to increase the probability students will learn, wonder about, and have passion for my content?

You don't need to answer this right away.
You don't need to write anything down.

Just notice what happens when you let the question sit with you
for a minute.

What part of this question feels most alive for you right now – your behavior, your lesson design, your students' learning, their wonder, or their passion?

When have you felt most proud of the way you showed up
for students?

If your classroom had a kind of north star, what would you hope
it was quietly pointing toward?

2 WHEN A QUESTION CHANGES THE ROOM

I was sitting with a group of teachers I had been asked to help. The request was clear enough: improve their productivity within the professional learning community structure – in other words, help fix a lagging, maybe broken team.

Back then, I did what I usually did.

I prepared.

I arrived with a PowerPoint on the finer points of professional learning communities – roles, norms, structures, protocols. Everything organized. Everything ready.

Before beginning the session, I decided to start with what felt like a simple question.

"What tasks are most worthy of the valuable investment of your limited time and efforts together?"

The room went silent.

Not polite silence.
Not thinking silence.

The kind of silence where something unexpected has landed. People shifted in their chairs. A few glanced down at the table. Someone tapped a pen lightly against a notebook.

I asked it again.

Still nothing.

Finally the team leader raised her hand.

"I don't think we know what you mean."

I remember pausing and looking around the room. I realized that the question had landed in a way I had not expected.

Then I reached over and closed the laptop.

The screen went black.

Something had shifted – and a very different conversation was about to begin.

I've always liked questions. Not the polite, transactional ones – "How are you?" or "Did everyone finish the assignment?" I mean the ones that don't quite let you go.

The kinds that follow you into the shower.
The kinds that show up when you're driving.
The questions that quietly return when something doesn't feel right.

Did everyone understand the directions?
Did we get through the material today?

Those are questions too. But they usually have short answers.

The questions that stay with you sound different.

Why did that moment with the students feel alive yesterday?
Why did the lesson before it feel flat?

What would it look like to design learning in a way that invites students into the thinking instead of just delivering it to them?

Those questions don't demand answers.

They create space.

And in that space, something can shift.

I didn't always think about questions this way. There was a time when I believed my job – in front of a group of students or teachers – was to arrive prepared with the right content, the right slides, and the right explanations. If I could be clear enough, precise enough, engaging enough, people would leave changed.

Sometimes they told me they did.

But somewhere along the way – I remember it being around 2004, in a big Missouri high school – I started noticing something unsettling. The sessions that were the most polished weren't always the ones that mattered most.

The charts were tidy, the data made sense, and the laughs landed.

And yet…

Very little actually moved.

What did seem to linger were quieter moments. Moments when someone said, "I hadn't thought about it that way before," or

"That makes me wonder about my own classroom."

I began paying attention to what came right before those moments.

Usually, it was a question.

Not a quiz question.
Not a rhetorical one.

Something open enough that people had to bring themselves into it.

"How does this idea land in your own classroom?"
"What part of this feels true for you?"
"How does this make sense in your context?"

Those questions didn't deliver answers.

They invited ownership.

Over time, I started trusting them more than my slides. When a real question was in the room, people leaned in differently. They spoke differently. They listened differently.

They didn't just collect information.

They made meaning.

That middle space – where you're not quite convinced and not ready to dismiss – has always felt like the most alive place to me. The place where you're not nodding and not yet turning away, but actually wondering.

That's what good questions do.

They don't tell you where to go.

They help you notice where you already are.

That's why questions sit at the heart of this book.

Not because I want to guide you.

But because I want to sit with you.

I'll share stories.
I'll name patterns I've seen.
I'll admit what I'm still wrestling with.

But none of that is the point.

The point is what happens when you begin to answer a question
for yourself in a soft voice.

You might agree with me.

You might not.

You might find yourself somewhere between – feeling both pulled
and unsettled.

And that's enough.

Pause and Reflect

Pause for a moment with the question that grew out of this chapter.

Essential Question
What is the purpose of essential questions?

You don't need to answer this right away. Just notice what happens when you let the question sit with you for a moment.

What's a question you've carried with you for a long time?

How do you tend to respond when someone asks something that doesn't have a clear answer?

If you had to frame your work around one big question, what might it be?

3 WHEN A QUESTION UNLOCKS WHAT STUDENTS ALREADY KNOW

I was working alongside a fourth-grade teacher as an instructional consultant when we began planning a lesson about angles. Before the lesson started, I asked her a simple question.

"What do you think the students already know?"

She paused for a moment and thought about it.

"Probably right angles," she said. "From squares and rectangles."

That seemed reasonable. So instead of beginning the lesson the way she had planned – by explaining angles from the beginning – we tried something different. We brought the students together at the front of the class asked them to turn and talk in pairs about one question:

"What is everything you know about angles?"

That was it. No diagram. No vocabulary. No definitions yet. Just the question.

At first the room sounded tentative. A few students leaned toward their partners and spoke quietly. One boy traced a corner in the air with his finger while he tried to explain something to the student beside him. Another student tilted her head, thinking, before whispering an idea to her partner.

Then the volume started to rise.

Soon the room was busy.

When we brought the class back together and invited students to share what they had discussed, something surprising happened. They talked about right angles. Then someone mentioned acute angles. Another student added obtuse angles. A few described angles as turns or corners. Several used their hands and arms to show what they meant.

Before long, they had named nearly everything we had planned to "teach" them that day.

Not because someone told them.

But because someone had asked them.

In that moment something became clear. The students didn't lack understanding the way we had assumed. What they lacked was an opening – an invitation to bring what they already knew into the room.

The problem wasn't knowledge.

It was access.

They didn't need to be filled.

They needed to be invited.

Watching those fourth-grade students claim so much of the learning themselves – working together, arguing about what made sense–

reminded me of moments in my own teaching when I had tried to explain too much.

And it hadn't landed.

I've been in education long enough to recognize a pattern in myself. When I'm nervous, I explain. When I'm trying to be helpful, I explain more. And when I deeply desire something to succeed, I can persuade myself that the right explanation will finally make everything click.

I've given those teacher workshops before. They're organized. Sometimes even engaging. People nod along. Occasionally they laugh in the right places. A few stay afterward to say thank you.

On the surface, it feels like success.

And yet something about those moments rarely lasts. The next day arrives, routines return, and the energy of the conversations gradually diminishes. It took me longer than I would like to admit to notice what was missing.

A good explanation can earn attention, and sometimes appreciation. But attention is not the same thing as learning.

Learning lives deeper than understanding a presenter or teacher's explanation.

If lecture alone were enough, deep learning would be far more common.

What you can do is ask a question that makes someone pause — something honest enough that people have to bring themselves into the conversation.

Then something interesting begins to happen: people start thinking and processing out loud.

Over time I began trusting those moments more than my explanations. When a genuine question entered the room, people leaned forward differently. They spoke with more ownership. They listened to one another in a different way.

They were no longer just collecting information.

They were actively exploring and making personal meaning.

Questions change posture. They slow people down enough to notice what they are assuming and what they might be overlooking. The most influential questions rarely arrive as polished sentences. They frequently appear sideways, as if by chance, during familiar routines.

What am I doing right now?

Why am I doing it this way?

What am I hoping will happen?

Is there a better way?

Those kinds of questions do not simply gather answers. They linger. They follow you into later moments – while planning a lesson, driving home after a long day, or sitting quietly after a class that did not unfold the way you expected.

Maybe that is the difference. What we say can be helpful, but what we ask can be catalytic.

Because a real question does not land like advice.

It lands like ownership.

Explanations can be useful and sometimes a critical component of learning. But when explanation becomes the primary engine of learning, students quietly learn that understanding is something delivered by the teacher and received by them.

Questions teach something different.

They teach that thinking belongs to the learner.

They teach that meaning making is something students build, not something they receive.

You've likely witnessed that moment firsthand. A student pauses, not in confusion, but in contemplation. They glance back at their work, reevaluating an idea, or reshaping their explanation for a classmate. It's a dance of thought, a spark of insight igniting their understanding.

It is the moment when the learning becomes theirs.

Which leaves me practicing a question of my own:

What changes in a classroom when we begin trusting questions more than telling?

Pause and Reflect

Pause for a moment with the question that grew out of this chapter.

Essential Question
Is it what we say or the questions we ask that have the most impact?

You don't need to answer this immediately. Just notice what happens when you let the question sit with you for a moment.

When was the last time a question changed the way you saw something?

Where in your teaching or leadership do you find yourself explaining when a question might invite deeper thinking?

What might become possible if learners – including yourself – were allowed to wrestle with ideas a little longer before someone stepped in to clarify?

4 WHEN LEARNING IS BUILT, NOT DELIVERED

I first heard the word constructivism in the early 2000s while sitting in a plastic chair at a round table in an old classroom washed in fluorescent light.

I was sitting in a graduate class at the University of Missouri–Kansas City, listening to a cherished professor, Dr. Larry Gregg. I don't remember the slides or the formal definitions he used that day. What I remember is the feeling – the quiet click when something inside me said, Oh… that's what's been going on.

Not a new idea – just a new way of naming something I had already experienced.

What Dr. Gregg shared helped me realize that learning doesn't happen because someone says the right thing – it happens when something finally makes sense, or doesn't, and you have to wrestle with it.

That felt true in my own life. It felt true watching six-year-olds stack blocks and argue about whose tower was taller. It felt true watching teenagers try to make sense of algebra. And it felt true sitting beside teachers who were rethinking their approaches to instruction.

Different ages.
Same process.

Meaning isn't delivered – it's built.

I've watched classrooms where students could repeat every step a teacher modeled and still have no idea what to do when the problem changed slightly.

And I've watched other rooms where students were confused at first – where they argued, tried things that didn't work, and had to explain themselves to one another. Those rooms were messier. Louder. Slower.

They were also more alive.

The students in those rooms didn't just get answers.

They got ownership.

You can feel it when it's happening. Kids lean forward in their chairs – someone erases their work and starts again. A student gestures with their hands while trying to explain an idea to a partner. Another pushes back with a soft tone: "Wait – I don't think that works."

The teacher isn't the center of attention any longer.

The thinking is.

Students look at each other instead of looking at the teacher. They try something risky. When they come back the next day, they don't just remember what they did – they think differently because of it.

That kind of learning leaves a residue – not just in school, but in the way people approach problems, relationships, and uncertainty long after they leave the classroom.

Of course, many of us were taught to teach in a way that sits in tension with this perspective on learning.

There's often a familiar rhythm to classrooms:

I do.
We do.
You do.

Gradual release makes sense – the teacher demonstrates, students practice, students try.

But over time I've started wondering about the order of those moves.

When do learners get their first chance to think for themselves?

I have a colleague – a science teacher and consultant named Anya – who plays with that question. She often begins not with explanation – not with modeling, but with a problem. Students try something. They talk. They get stuck. They make sense together. She listens, asks questions, and gives hints. She gathers information that drives her instructional decisions in real time.

Only later does she step in as the expert to summarize and formalize the learning.

It isn't perfect. It isn't always clean.

But it's honest.

It lets students feel what it's like to be inside a question before someone hands them a solution.

Only then do we name it.

That way of seeing and experiencing learning – at least as I've come to understand it – is the heart of constructivism.

Not a method or a program – but a stance: a belief that learning grows from struggle, curiosity, conversation, and time.

Which brings me back to the question that keeps following me:

What changes in a classroom when we start trusting a messier learning process a little more?

Pause and Reflect

Pause for a moment with the question that grew out of this chapter.

Essential Question
What is constructivism – and why should I care?

You don't need to answer this immediately. Just notice what happens when you let the question sit with you for a moment.

When have you learned something deeply without being taught directly?

Where might your students need more room to struggle, try, and make sense?

What would it look like to trust the learning process just a little more?

5 HOW TO LIVE WITH THIS BOOK

I've always believed that questions do their best work when they're shared.

Not in neat, polite conversations – but in the messy ones. The kind where people disagree, where stories spill out, where no one quite knows what the right answer is.

Some of the richest moments I've seen in schools didn't come from polished presentations. They came from teachers sitting in small circles, trying to make sense of something together.

That's how I imagine this book living – on a table between people. A grade-level team. A book club. A professional learning community. Or a couple of colleagues who trust each other enough to be honest.

Of course, you might be reading on your own.

That's okay too.

Sometimes the quiet conversation inside your own head is exactly what's needed. Still, I can't help wondering what might happen if someone spoke some of these questions out loud – if another got to say, "That's not how it feels to me."

When I hold this book in my hands, I sometimes worry about how it looks.

Questions. Reflections. Invitations to think.

It could be mistaken for a how-to book – or worse, a self-help book that promises favorable outcomes if you follow the steps.

That isn't what I'm offering.

This book is a companion – something to walk beside you while you keep doing the hard, quiet work of teaching.

There's no right way to move through these pages.

You might linger in one chapter for weeks.

You might skip around.

You might write in the margins.

You might feel annoyed by something and come back to it later, surprised.

All that counts.

The only thing I ask is that you don't rush past the places that make you pause.

That's usually where something is trying to happen.

So maybe the real question isn't how to use this book.

It's who you'll be while you're reading it.

Pause and Reflect

Pause for a moment with the question that grew out of this chapter.

Essential Question
How can I use this book?

You might sit with this question before moving on.

Who might you want beside you as you read?

What part of your practice feels most alive – or most unsettled – right now?

If one small change came from this book, what would you hope it would be?

WHEN QUESTIONS MEET STUDENTS

Across these opening chapters, we've spent time living with questions – noticing how they change the way we see the work.

A question found me in Kathy's empty classroom.
Another stopped a presentation before it even began.
Others appeared in classrooms where students started thinking out loud instead of waiting for answers.

None of those moments came from a strategy.

They came from a shift in attention – from delivering ideas to noticing what was already happening in the room.

Questions have a way of doing that. They slow us down just enough to see what's happening. We notice our assumptions, our habits, and the possibilities we might miss.

This first part was meant to accomplish that.

Not to give you a system.
Not to offer a framework.

To help you pause long enough to notice the questions that already live inside your work.

Because once those questions start appearing, something else becomes harder to ignore.

Teaching isn't only about ideas.

It's about people.

Students arrive every day with histories we can't see, strengths we haven't discovered yet, and uncertainties they rarely say out loud. The questions we carry shape the way we design learning, but they also shape something even more fundamental.

They shape how we show up with students.

Whether students feel safe enough to try.
Whether they feel seen enough to speak.
Whether they believe they belong inside the work of learning.

That's where the next set of questions lives.

Not in curriculum.
Not in strategies.
Not in lesson plans.

In relationships.

Before students wrestle with ideas, they first answer another question in silence:

Is it safe for me to try here?

And the answer to that question has a lot to do with how we behave with them.

PART 2

BUILDING RELATIONSHIPS
HOW STUDENTS EXPERIENCE WHO WE ARE.

WHAT THE TEACHER IS, IS MORE IMPORTANT
THAN WHAT HE TEACHES.
KARL MENNINGER

6 WHERE RESILIENCE BEGINS

One afternoon a student sat down across from me and said,

"Brooks… I need to drop AP Bio."

I asked what she wanted to be someday.

"A dermatologist."

We talked for a while about science, college, and how this was the
first class that had ever truly knocked her off balance. About how
her 4.0 suddenly felt fragile. About how quitting felt safer than
staying.

At some point she said,

"I'll be ready for med school."

She sounded certain about the future – and terrified of the present.

I didn't have a clever answer for her. I didn't have a formula. But I
kept circling one quiet idea:

If you leave when it gets hard, you never learn that you can stay.

For nearly a decade, I sat behind a desk as an assistant principal, engaging in variations of that same conversation.

The faces changed - the stories didn't

"It's hard."
"I don't have time."
"My teacher isn't helping me."
"I'm lost."
"I'm so behind."
"But my GPA…"

By the time students made it to my office, they weren't only frustrated. They were exhausted, scared, and quietly convinced they were about to fail at something that mattered.

I was usually the last stop before they could drop a class.

Some students did leave.
Some stayed.

But every so often one would come back months later and say something like,

"I'm glad I didn't drop it."

Not because it got easy.

But because they got stronger.

Over the years I found myself saying something similar to students again and again.

"This class has more to teach you than the content."

At first they usually looked confused. They assumed I meant the content would prepare them for college or a future profession. But that wasn't what I meant. The content was only the surface of something else.

Classes like that teach something else – something quieter and harder to measure.

They teach what it feels like to stay when things stop being easy.

They teach how to keep working when confidence wobbles, and they teach that confusion isn't always a signal to leave.

Sometimes it's a signal that you're exactly where learning lives.

I noticed something simple: most students don't quit due to inability. They quit because they think struggle means something is wrong with them.

Many students pick up the idea that learning should be easy. If they find something hard, confusing, or frustrating, they think it means they're not smart enough. So when the first real academic struggle arrives, it feels less like learning and more like failure.

What students need most in those moments isn't a clever explanation or a quick solution.

What they need is someone who isn't done with them yet.

Someone who can hold the possibility of being stronger than they currently feel. Resilience grows there – in the places where it would be easier to leave.

And sometimes it grows just because someone says,

"You can stay."

Pause and Reflect

Pause for a moment with the question that grew out of this chapter.

Essential Question
How do I encourage resilience in my students?

You don't need to answer this right away. Just notice what happens when you let the question sit with you for a moment.

When was the last time you wanted to quit something that mattered to you?

Who believed in you when things felt hard?

What do you do – or not do – when a student is right on the edge of giving up?

7 THEY REMEMBER WHAT WE WERE

I keep coming back to one part of the essential question that anchors this book: How will I behave with my students?

Not what will I teach.

Not what strategies will I use.

But who will I be when they walk into the room each day?

I used to think relationships were something you built on top of good teaching – like an extra layer. Now they're the ground everything else stands on.

Students don't just hear what we say.
They feel what we are.

Years ago I came across a quote from Jim Henson that captured this idea perfectly. I misremembered it at first – I thought it ended with something about caring. But the actual line was simpler and sharper:

"They remember what you are."

That line stayed with me. It made me wonder what my students were remembering about me – even on days when I wasn't trying to teach anything at all.

I once went to a workshop in a busy hotel conference room. The presenter wrote three key messages on a whiteboard. He thought students should hear these every day:

"This is important."
"I know you can do it."
"I will not give up on you."

They sounded almost too simple.

But I started paying attention to how often – or how rarely – those ideas were actually communicated and felt in a classroom. So I tried to live them.

Sometimes it showed up in what I said. Sometimes in what I didn't rush to fix. Sometimes it showed up in how long I stayed beside a student who was stuck.

At one point I put those three statements on a poster. At first it felt a little cheesy. But over time it stopped being decoration and became something I practiced almost unconsciously.

There was another idea I often shared with my students that mattered to me.

"In this class, we are either learning or confirming. If you get it right, you confirm your understanding. If you get it wrong, you learn. Both count."

I didn't say it because it sounded clever.

I said it because I needed it to be true.

The classroom underwent a gradual change.

Students stopped apologizing for not knowing. They raised their hands when they weren't sure. The confident ones learned how to listen, and the quiet ones found their voices.

Nothing about the curriculum was different.

But the air was.

In that space – where it was safe to be unfinished – something provided learning a place to land. Not because of what I taught, but because of what I stood for.

That's the part of teaching I keep coming back to.

When a learner walks into a room, they are always asking a quiet question.

Who is this teacher, and what does it mean to be here?

Our answer isn't only in our words. It exists in the atmosphere we create, in how we respond when someone struggles, and in whether students believe they are allowed to continue becoming.

Over time, students don't just remember what we taught.
They remember what we were.

Pause and Reflect

Pause for a moment with the question that grew out of this chapter.

Essential Question
What do I stand for?

You don't need to answer this right away. Just notice what happens when you let the question sit with you for a moment.

What do you hope students feel when they enter your room?

What do you want them to believe about themselves when they leave?

If someone watched you teach for a week, what might they say you stand for?

8 THE ECHO OF BEING SEEN

I still remember where I was in the fall of 1985.

Algebra II. Third row. Helping the kids around me when they were stuck.

I was pretty good at math, and my teacher – Mrs. McNary – knew it. She often encouraged me to help classmates while she worked her way around the room.

One day she asked me to stay after class. That alone made my stomach drop. Staying after class was never good news.

"Billy," she said, "you know how I sometimes ask you to help others?"

"Sure. I like helping."

"Well, today I listened."

I waited while she continued. She told me she had listened while I helped three different groups of students with the same problem, and that I approached it in a unique way each time. I hadn't told them what to do – I had asked questions and helped them think.

I remember staring at her for a moment before asking, "So… I'm not in trouble?"

She smiled.

"Not at all. I don't know what you plan to do with your life, but if you ever thought about being a math teacher, that's a good thought. You'd be really good at it."

That was it.

Two minutes. One conversation.

We didn't become close. I didn't stay after class again. I didn't share my personal life with her. We didn't have a special relationship.

But something inside me shifted.

Someone had noticed me – not what I did, but who I was becoming.

And I carried that with me.

Years later, after I had become a teacher myself, I started to realize how rare those moments actually are. How many students move through classrooms feeling invisible. How often teachers see work instead of people.

Noticing isn't dramatic.

It doesn't require crossing boundaries. It doesn't require sharing lives. It doesn't take much time.

It requires paying attention – and then saying what you saw.

"You helped someone."

"You didn't give up."

"You tried a different way."

"You asked a good question."

Those small moments land deeper than we think.

Somewhere along the way, many teachers stop seeing only content and start also seeing people. And when that happens, something changes.

Learning feels safer.

Struggle feels less lonely.

Possibility feels closer.

Noticing is quiet, but it echoes.

Sometimes for a lifetime.

Pause and Reflect

Pause for a moment with the question that grew out of this chapter.

Essential Question
What is the power of noticing?

You don't need to answer this right away. Just notice what happens when you let the question sit with you for a moment.

Who was the first adult who really saw you?

Which student in your world might need to be noticed right now?

What might change if you said out loud what you already see?

9 THE LESSON BENEATH THE LESSON

There's a sign in one of the schools I worked with that reads:

Relationships before rigor.

Not everyone hears that the same way.

Over the years, teachers have said things like:

"I'm not touchy-feely."
"I don't share my personal life."
"I don't want to blur lines."
"I just love the content."

I understand that.

I believe it.

One of my early mentors, Kristel Barr, who had a way of cutting through nonsense, used to say, "You can teach skills. You can't change personalities. The only things that change personalities are religious conversions, psychotherapy, and lobotomies… and we don't offer any of those here."

She was joking.

Mostly.

But what she meant stayed with me.

You don't have to become someone else to matter to students. You don't have to change your personality. You don't have to perform warmth or turn your classroom into a living room.

You just have to recognize that someone is always teaching something – even when it isn't on the syllabus.

Years ago, after a workshop on relationships, a teacher stayed behind to talk. He was openly skeptical and uneasy about the whole idea. He believed that "relationship-building" meant crossing lines he didn't want to cross.

But something had shifted.

We started talking not about personalities, but about messages.

What message did his classroom convey to students each day?

Not through what he taught – but through how he taught.

I realized that was true for me too. Whether I meant to or not, my students were always learning something about themselves in my room:

That what we were doing mattered, and that struggling was part of thinking.
That confusion wasn't failure – it was information.
That effort connected to what happened next.

I wasn't just teaching concepts and skills. I taught what it's like to struggle with something tough and keep going. It's about seeing the gap between what you think you know and what you really know. It's also about trying again.

None of that required a bubbly personality.

It required being intentional about what was being communicated beneath the surface.

I've observed teachers who never mentioned feelings create classrooms where trust flourished because their routines conveyed the message, You belong here.

I've watched others who never shared their personal lives still send the message, I care about who you are becoming.

That's when I realized something that changed me:

Relationships aren't built by who you pretend to be.

They're built by what you demonstrate over time.

Which makes me wonder about something I still wrestle with:

What are students learning about themselves in my room… even when I'm focused on content?

Pause and Reflect

Pause for a moment with the question that grew out of this chapter.

Essential Question
What non-curricular messages am I sending?

You don't need to answer this right away. Just notice what happens when you let the question sit with you for a moment.

What are students really learning from the way you run your classroom?

What do your routines, tone, and responses quietly teach them about themselves?

If your class left one lasting message, what would you hope it would be?

10 THE LANGUAGE OF BELONGING

A few years ago, I visited my oldest daughter while she was in law school.
She walked me through her campus at George Washington University – past historic buildings, down into basement law libraries, and along rows of classrooms. But the place that has stayed with me is an unassuming, medium-sized lecture hall she made sure we passed through.

We stopped and looked around.

And then she told me a story.

It was her first week of law school. She had buried herself in case readings. Her professor in that room called on students unexpectedly. They had to explain choices, defend ideas, and think out loud in front of the class.
And there was something else. The professor seemed to enjoy putting students on the spot in front of fifty of their peers – not to embarrass them, but because he knew they needed it. They needed to sit in the discomfort – to wrestle with language and think in real time. It was part of becoming an attorney.

She told me about the day he called on her.

She stood up in front of her peers.

He questioned her about a case.

She responded.

He pushed back.

She tried again.

And in that back-and-forth – nervous, imperfect, and public – something began to shift.

"I sounded like a lawyer for the first time," she told me. "And it was awesome!"

She wasn't talking about getting it right.

She was talking about belonging.

That story stayed with me.

Back in my own classroom – long before that visit – I had heard a different sentence over and over.

"I don't get it."

For years, I thought that was about content. About math. About ability.

I eventually came to understand that it
was frequently about language.

Students didn't just need to understand the content – they needed to be able to speak it.

I started designing my lessons around a quieter question:

How can I help my students talk like mathematicians?

Not perfectly.

Not confidently at first.

Just enough to try.

I began paying closer attention to how my students spoke – the words they reached for, the pauses, the half-formed ideas. I gave them more chances to try out the language, even when it came out crooked. I honored their attempts to make sense of the content verbally.

And slowly, something shifted.

More voices entered the room.

Quieter students took small risks.

A term here.
An idea there.
A sentence that almost worked.

As their language grew and became more accurate, so did their confidence. And as their confidence grew, so did their connection – to me, to the class, and to the work.

I used to think I was helping by modeling correct language and correcting student language swiftly.

What I learned was that helping students find the language mattered more than correcting them right away. I made it okay to work slowly toward the accuracy and precision of our content vocabulary.

Because when a student finally has the words to speak, something changes.

They don't just understand more.

They belong more.

Pause and Reflect

Pause for a moment with the question that grew out of this chapter.

Essential Question
How can supporting academic and content language in my classroom help build relationships?

You don't need to answer this right away. Just notice what happens when you let the question sit with you for a moment.

When was the last time you felt confident because you finally had the words?

Which students in your world don't yet have the language to belong?

What might it look like to invite them into the conversation more fully?

HOW WE SHOW UP SHAPES WHAT WE DESIGN

Across these chapters, I've shared a handful of ways I've tried to show up for students – not as a personality type, but as a person who believes learning happens best when people feel seen, safe, and capable.

None of these are tricks. They're choices about how to be with students when things get hard, confusing, or uncomfortable.

And that's what relationships in a classroom come down to: how you show up when it matters.

Sometimes it shows up in how you respond when learning gets difficult.
Sometimes in what students feel from you each day.
Sometimes in the quiet act of noticing who a student is becoming, or in the messages your routines send about belonging and possibility.

The questions in this part all live inside the same larger one:

How will I behave with my students?

There isn't one right answer.

But there are always consequences – for trust, for risk-taking, and for whether students feel like they belong.

Which leads us to the next topic.

Once you decide how you want to be with students, the next question is unavoidable:

How will you design learning to match that?

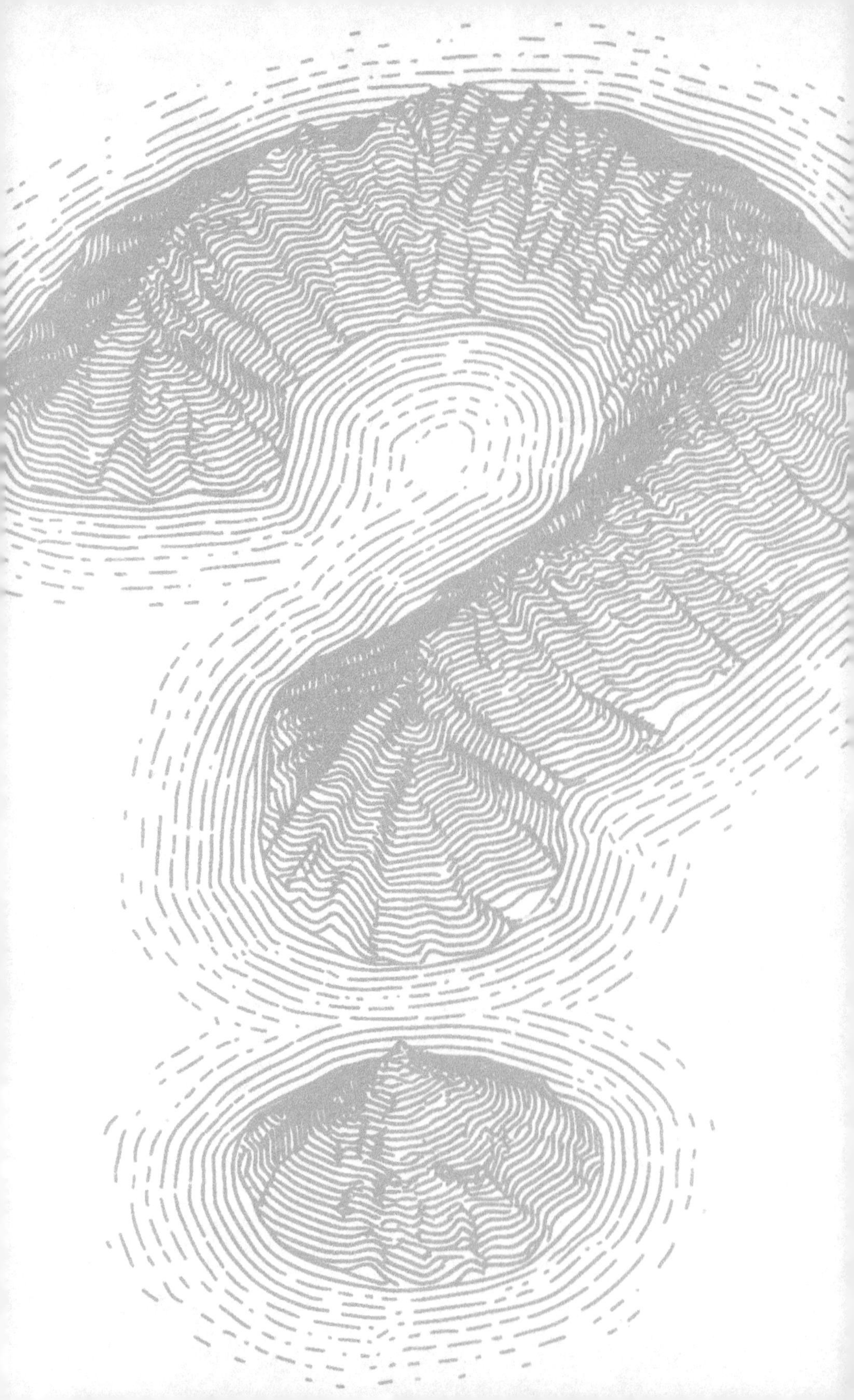

PART 3

○

DESIGNING LEARNING

HOW WE SHAPE EXPERIENCES
WHERE THINKING CAN EMERGE.

○

THE TEACHER'S TASK IS NOT TO IMPART KNOWLEDGE,
BUT TO CREATE THE CONDITIONS FOR ITS DISCOVERY.
SEYMOUR PAPERT

11 WHEN LEARNING HAS A STORY

Once, I taught a course called Preparation for College Algebra. The students were nervous and convinced they didn't belong there. And certainly not in the next course – College Algebra.

On the first day I told them the story I saw.

"This class is a story that consists of four chapters," I said. "We're going to do a lot of the same math, but the world keeps changing. First, the exponents stay at one. Then they grow. Then they become fractions. And then, things get strange and imaginary."

It wasn't poetry, but it was a story.

And I kept returning to it.

What we'd already seen.
What was coming.
Where things were about to get weird.

Sometimes I added math history. Sometimes a personal struggle from my own learning. Sometimes I invited students into the story – to invent scenarios with me – choosing cars, loans, down payments, and watching how the math changed the story.

What I noticed wasn't subtle.

Students paid attention differently. They asked better questions.
They made predictions.
And most of all, they stayed.

One afternoon near the end of my last full year in the classroom, a
student stayed after.

"Brooks! It feels like you're talking directly to me when you teach,"
she said. "I don't know how you do that. But I'm really into it."

I didn't know how to answer her.

But later, walking to my car, I realized what she had felt.

She knew where she was in the story. And she was a character in
the story.

When a lesson, chapter, or unit has a story, it doesn't just teach.

It invites someone in.

Everything that follows in this part of the book lives inside a simple
truth:

How we design learning can't be separated from how we show up
for people.

Every class, every unit, every lesson is part of a story – whether we
mean it to be or not.

Sometimes it's a story students can feel themselves inside. Other
times it's just a stack of scenes that never quite connect.

I didn't always notice the difference.

There were years when I walked into a classroom with nothing but confidence and called it preparation. I used to say things like, "Give me any Algebra 1 topic and I can build a 90-minute lesson on the spot."

That was true.

But it wasn't enough.

I didn't start planning in a new way because someone told me to. I started because I could feel something missing in the room when I didn't. Students were doing the work, but they weren't inside anything larger than the moment.

And people need stories.

I began to ask quieter questions when planning lessons:

Where are we in the story right now?
What just happened?
What's about to happen?
Where is the tension?
Where is the big reveal?

Those questions changed the way I designed learning.

Pause and Reflect

Pause for a moment with the question that grew out of this chapter.

Essential Question
How can designing learning as a story help students stay engaged and connected to the work?

You don't need to answer this right away. Just notice what happens when you let the question sit with you for a moment.

Where are your students right now in the story of your course – beginning, stuck, or on the edge of something new?

When have you felt most connected to a lesson you were teaching? What made it feel alive?

If your students could describe today's lesson as part of a larger journey, what would they say it was about?

12 **STOP TEACHING BLIND**

Fall of 1992.

I was sitting at my desk staring at a stack of quizzes that made my stomach drop. Five classes. Almost no A's. Barely any B's. Two full weeks of teaching – gone. Or at least that's how it felt.

I remember thinking that I had explained all of it – slowly, carefully, clearly.

So I went to a friend in the department, confused and more than a little shaken.

"I don't know where I went wrong," I told him. "I explained everything."

He listened for a moment and then asked a small question that ended up changing a lot.

"Have you ever used exit tickets?"

I hadn't.

He explained how I could ask one or two questions at the end of class to get a quick snapshot of what students were thinking before they walked out the door. I tried it, and it helped. For a while it felt like I had found the answer.

But then I realized something uncomfortable.

The end of class was still too late.

If I honestly cared about learning – not just getting through material – I needed to know what students were thinking while it was happening, not after the potential damage was already done.

Back then, I thought being a great explainer was the job. But explanation only tells you what you know through a performance. It doesn't tell you what they are thinking.

Over the next few decades I tried about everything: clickers, whiteboards, thumbs up, fists of five, tech tools that promised instant data. Some of it helped.

But nothing really changed until I stopped trying to collect answers and started trying to watch and listen to student thinking.

Near the end of my time in the classroom, colleagues introduced me to routines designed to make thinking visible – not from the confident few, but from all students. The first time I used them well, it felt like someone had handed me a pair of glasses I didn't know I was missing.

I wasn't guessing anymore.

I could hear ideas forming.
I could see misunderstandings taking shape.
I could feel where the room was going – and where it wasn't.

One day I watched a first-year history teacher review the Industrial Revolution by organizing small groups and selecting prompts with great care. Students weren't answering questions quickly. They were talking their way through ideas.

At one table a student said, "Wait… if factories made things faster and were so great, why were people still poor?"

Another replied, "Maybe the factory owners kept most of the money."

A third added, "So the machines helped some people but hurt others."

The teacher didn't interrupt. She listened and asked a few careful questions.

As I walked the room, it was all there.

What they knew.
What they didn't.
What they were trying to figure out.

No interruptions.
No raised hands.
No hiding.

Just thinking, out loud.

And that's when it finally landed for me:

Knowing what students are thinking isn't always about speed, efficiency, or technology.

It's about creating conditions where their thinking must surface.

When that happens, you stop teaching blind.

You start walking alongside students instead of guessing.

And students stop performing and start showing you who they are as learners.

I wish I had understood that back in 1992.

Pause and Reflect

Pause for a moment with the question that grew out of this chapter.

Essential Question
How will I know what all my students are thinking as soon as possible?

You don't need to answer this right away. Just notice what happens when you let the question sit with you for a moment.

When was the last time you really knew what most of your students were thinking in the middle of a lesson? What made that possible?

Whose thinking do you hear most easily in your classroom – and whose do you rarely hear at all?

What might change if tomorrow's lesson were designed around listening instead of explaining?

13 WHILE THE MEANING IS STILL WARM

Here's the thing: I used to plan to summarize learning at the end of every lesson.

I knew exactly how it would sound. I knew how it would connect back to our goal. It was going to be that neat reflective moment that tied everything together.

And then the bell would ring. Or I hadn't collected supplies in time.

Over and over again.

There was always more to do than there was time. I valued summarizing and consolidating student learning, but it often felt like a hope rather than a reality.

That began to change when I started paying closer attention to what my students were thinking during class.

As their thinking became more visible and more audible, I noticed something I had missed for years:

Some of the most important learning wasn't happening at the end of the lesson.

It was happening in the middle.

One day in Algebra 1, I observed different groups solving the same equation using different methods, and each group arrived at the correct solution.

And something in me said, "Everyone needs to see this."

Not later.

Now.

So I stopped the class.

"Time out, everyone. I've got something pretty cool to show you."

We walked from group to group, looking at the strategies students had used. We talked about the approach they chose and the decisions they made. Students asked questions. They noticed patterns. They saw how thinking could move in different directions and still land somewhere true.

That moment changed how I thought about summarizing forever.

I used to believe you summarized when you were finished. Teach. Wrap it up. Let the bell send everyone on their way.

But what changed wasn't my planning.

It was my watching and listening.

When I began to understand what students were thinking, I realized that summarizing isn't always about closure.

It's about timing.

Sometimes you summarize at the beginning.

Sometimes at the end.

But the most powerful summaries happen when ideas are still warm – when confusion, insight, and curiosity are all in the room together. That's when learning becomes shared. That's when students start to not only see where they are, but what it means.

Over time I found myself carrying a few quiet questions as I planned:

Is there something worth revisiting at the beginning?

Where might I anticipate moments to pause and make sense together?

What moments might be worth stopping for?

And if something unexpected shows up – will I notice it? Will I be watching with intention?

Most importantly:

How will I be an active learner of what my students are thinking?

When I began searching for those in-the-middle moments, the room changed.

Conversations deepened.

Ideas traveled.

Understanding grew.

Summarizing stopped being an ending.

It became part of the journey.

Pause and Reflect

Pause for a moment with the question that grew out of this chapter.

Essential Question
When should I summarize learning?

You don't need to answer this right away. Just notice what happens when you let the question sit with you for a moment.

When have you seen understanding grow because someone paused the class and named what was happening?

Where in your own lessons do ideas seem to come alive – even if the bell hasn't rung yet?

What might change if you trusted those moments enough to stop and make sense together?

14 HOPE IS NOT A PLAN

I spent years getting my students busy.

And it felt good.

And honestly, I was pretty good at it.

Principals loved the buzz in my room. Students were working. Heads were down. Pencils were moving. Pages were turning. Someone would erase something in a hurry and start again. It looked exactly like what learning was supposed to look like.

They were doing the activity.
They were on task.
They were working.

Right?

Then the assessments came back, and I was almost never as happy as I thought I should be.

With a sense of discomfort, I gradually came to a realization:

I had been overestimating what they understood.

They had looked busy.
I had felt successful.

And I had too often been wrong.

Does any of that sound familiar?

For a long time I lived in what I now think of as the space between busy and hope.

I hoped the work they were doing was turning into understanding.
I hoped the conversations they were having were about the
right things.
I hoped the answers they were writing meant what I thought they
meant.

Sometimes hope was enough.

Often it wasn't.

Early in my career, I had a department mentor and a co-teacher who subtly influenced my thinking. We were standing in the middle of a room full of students working when he said something that stuck with me.

"It's not enough that they're busy. We have to know if they're actually learning."

That line followed me for the rest of my career.

Busy isn't bad.

But busy without actively watching and listening is dangerous.

What I learned over time is that lesson design and verification must coexist. It isn't enough to give students something to do. I have to be in the room while they're doing it – observing, sensing, and adjusting.

That represented a distinct moment when my approach to effective teaching took a step forward.

I stopped designing lessons that made me feel good and started designing lessons that let me know what students understood.

I wanted students talking – not just working.

I wanted to hear how they were making sense of things.

I wanted to see where their thinking broke down.

And I wanted the chance to respond while it still mattered.

So when I plan now, I'm not only asking,

"What will they do?"

I'm asking,

"How will I know what they are thinking?"

That shift – coupling activity with awareness – was everything.

So what went wrong in all those busy rooms I once felt so good about?

Nothing… exactly.

But I was relying on hope.

And hope is a fragile thing to build learning upon.

What changed me was making a commitment to verify – to actually see and hear what students were doing with the work I put in front of them.

That's when I stopped teaching activities

and started teaching learners.

Pause and Reflect

Pause for a moment with the question that grew out of this chapter.

Essential Question
What is wrong with a busy classroom?

You don't need to answer this right away. Just notice what happens when you let the question sit with you for a moment.

When students are working in your room, how do you usually decide whether real learning is happening? What are you looking and listening for?

Think of a recent lesson that felt productive. What did you know about student understanding during that time, and what were your main hopes?

What's one small way you could design tomorrow's lesson so you can see or hear students' thinking instead of having to guess?

15 THE RHYTHM OF TEACHING

I've spent a lot of time in classrooms – beautiful ones, messy ones, and everything between.

Most lessons I see aren't broken. They work. But many of them are sitting right on the edge of something better.

As an instructional coach at a big highschool with thirteen departments and nearly a hundred teachers, I witnessed every kind of teaching. Some teachers paced the aisles, hands motioning in the air as they explained ideas. Others barely turned from the board, chalk racing across it while students copied quietly. Some classrooms hummed with conversation. Others were almost silent.

No two rooms were the same.

And yet, over time, I started noticing something.

In classrooms where thinking really came alive, a certain rhythm often appeared – a kind of back-and-forth movement between teacher and learner. Not a formula. Not a script. More like the steps of a dance where someone leads for a moment, then steps aside so someone else can move or even lead.

When that rhythm showed up, learning seemed to move forward.

It often looked something like this.

The First Five Minutes Matter.
One prompt. One problem. One invitation into the work. Often something that builds or reignites students' background knowledge.

Mini-lesson.
A teacher explains, models, or sets direction – short enough that students still have space to think. Usually a 2-10 minute mini-lesson is all it took.

Students Work.
In individual tasks, in pairs, or in groups. This is where the teacher gets to watch and listen.

Catch-and-Release.
The room comes back together for a moment. A teacher highlights something worth noticing, surfaces an idea, or nudges the thinking. Maybe another mini-lesson is needed.

Back to Work.
Students try again. They test their thinking.

Another catch-and-release.
Ideas get connected. Misconceptions surface. Someone's thinking helps the room move forward.

Application.
A new problem. A deeper stretch. Something that pushes learning a little further.

Summarize.
The class revisits the goal. Patterns are named. Meaning is made together.

The timing of this rhythm changes.

Some days are test days. Others are lab days.. Some days introduce brand-new content, while others focus on review.

The point isn't following a script. The point is noticing when thinking is alive – and inviting students into it.

When that happens, the classroom begins to feel different. Students are on their toes and more engaged. Teachers watch and listen more. Ideas move around the room instead of staying at the front.

And the lesson stops feeling like someone is delivering it. It starts to feel like something unfolding.

Like a dance.

Sometimes the teacher leads. Sometimes the students do. But the movement goes back and forth – each responding to the other.

That's the craft. That's the art inside lesson design.

When it works, it feels like teaching again.

Not managing.
Not performing.

Teaching.

Pause and Reflect

Pause for a moment with the question that grew out of this chapter.

Essential Question

How can I upgrade my lesson design during the year?

You don't need to answer this right away. Just notice what happens when you let the question sit with you for a moment.

When you picture one of your best class periods, what is happening between you and your students?

Where in your lessons do students get their first real chance to think for themselves?

If learning in your classroom felt more like a rhythm or a dance, what might shift in the way you move between explaining, listening, and responding?

What is one small adjustment you could try tomorrow that might invite more of that movement?

16 **BACK INTO CURIOSITY**

The school year eventually reaches a moment when something shifts. The daylight fades earlier. The semester stretches longer than it seemed in August, and routines that once felt helpful begin to feel a little heavy.

You're still showing up. The students are still showing up.

But the spark isn't quite what it was at the beginning of the year.

In moments like that, teachers often look for something big – a new strategy, a new program, a new plan that will somehow reset the room.

But sometimes the shift comes from something smaller.

Not a full redesign.

A few questions that help you gain a different perspective on your classroom.

These are three questions I find myself returning to when things start to feel stale. Not because they fix everything, but because they help me notice what's really happening.

Question #1: How are my students making sense of ideas by speaking?

Every classroom has a few students who can learn no matter how you teach. They take notes. They recognize patterns. They do school beautifully.

But this question isn't really about them.

It's about everyone else.

Most students don't make full sense of ideas only by listening.

They need to say things. They need to try language out loud. They need to stumble through an idea once or twice before it begins to make sense.

When students talk – to each other, in pairs, in small groups, or with the teacher – something changes.

Thinking slows down enough to become audible.

Instead of simply receiving ideas, students begin shaping them.

Sometimes the most powerful move a teacher can make is this:

Don't say the thing yet.

Let them talk their way toward, around, and through it.

Question #2: How am I mobilizing student thinking?

An active classroom – one where students are talking and exploring ideas – can feel uncomfortable at first.

Teachers worry about missing something important. They worry about students getting things wrong. They worry about losing control of the room.

That's where consolidation matters.

While students work, you watch and listen.

You notice patterns.

You hear misconceptions.

You give hints or extensions to ideas and concepts.

You spot good ideas emerging in different corners of the room.

And then, at the right moment, you pause the class.

"Let's look at what happened over here."

Students still get to wrestle with ideas.

They just don't have to wrestle alone.

Question #3: Is it time to try something again?

Most good strategies don't feel good the first time.

The mechanics come first.

The nuance takes longer.

We sometimes make hasty decisions about whether a strategy does or does not work.

But often what didn't work wasn't the idea itself – it was that we hadn't yet learned how to use it well.

Is there something you tried once that still lingers in the back of your mind?

Something that felt promising, even if it was messy?

Sometimes growth begins by revisiting an idea with a little more patience than we had the first time.

These three questions aren't magic.

But they do something important.

They pull you back into curiosity.

They ask you to notice instead of rush.

And sometimes, in the long middle of a school year, that's exactly what a classroom needs.

Pause and Reflect

Pause for a moment with the question that grew out of this chapter.

Essential Question
What are quick ways to improve my instruction tomorrow?

You don't need to answer this right away. Just notice what happens when you let the question sit with you for a moment.

Where in your classroom do students get to think out loud – and where do they mostly just listen?

When was the last time you paused a lesson to make sense of what your students were discovering together?

Is there a strategy you once set aside that might deserve another look now that you're a little different than you were then?

17 WHAT TECHNOLOGY MAKES POSSIBLE

The summer of 2015 found me in a loud, chaotic cafeteria, packed with students picking up their schedules.

I was a new assistant principal at a high school of about 1,700 students. I stood near a long line of parents and students. Kids picked up schedules, forms, and laptops. Parents handled signatures – and opened checkbooks to pay fees and settle fines.

There was something different about this day. For the first time, every student in the building was receiving an electronic device – a laptop.

A teacher from our leadership team came up beside me and watched it all unfold.

"I wish we would have received more training on this," she said. "I don't know how I'm supposed to handle technology in my classroom. This is going to be interesting."

She wasn't being sarcastic. She was being honest.

And she was right.

We were rolling out a massive shift in how learning could happen, and most of us were being asked to figure it out on the fly. So we did what schools often do when the ground shifts: we tried to keep up.

We started building the plane in the air.

Our principal was brave. He didn't prescribe how devices should be used, and he didn't panic. He trusted teachers to teach students how to use them. Some classrooms figured it out beautifully. Others did not.

We tried to help by sharing management ideas, discussing courtesy closes, and swapping stories – and that part mattered.

But then something subtle happened.

We drifted.

Instead of talking about learning, we started training teachers on tools.

Apps. Extensions. Platforms.

And that's when things began to unravel.

If a tool happened to fit what you were teaching, great. If it didn't, you sat through another training anyway.

The breaking point came the day we asked teachers to give up their planning time again to learn about technology.

I still remember the text message that landed on my phone:

"Really? I lost my prep to learn how to make a cute meme?"

We weren't talking about learning anymore.

We were talking about toys.

In the next technology task force meeting, we could all feel it – the frustration, the fatigue, the sense that we were missing something obvious. Someone mentioned a framework. Someone else mentioned a model.

None of it answered the question that teachers were genuinely asking.

What does this mean for my students tomorrow?

I stood up, walked to the board, and wrote a single sentence.

If not for the laptops in my classroom, my students would have never been able to ______________.

The room went quiet.

That sentence didn't ask about tools.

It asked about possibilities.

When we shared it with teachers, their answers changed everything.

"My students were able to visit a museum they'll never see in person."

"My class talked live with an author across the country."

"My kids ran experiments we could never afford to run."

We ultimately expanded the question.

If not for ____________________, my students would have never been able to ____________________.

That question became a compass. Whenever technology felt distracting or overwhelming, I came back to it. If it didn't open a door that couldn't be opened another way, it didn't belong.

Over time teachers didn't become experts in every tool, but they became clearer about why they were using them. They tried things, failed, and tried again – and the stories began to pile up.

That's what technology is for.

Not flash.
Not compliance.

It's for making something possible that wasn't before.

So now, when I think about using technology in the classroom, I don't start with tools.

I start with a different question:

What do I want my students to experience?

And then I see if technology can help make that story real.

Pause and Reflect

Pause for a moment with the question that grew out of this chapter.

Essential Question
How will I incorporate technology into my classroom?

You don't need to answer this right away. Just notice what happens when you let the question sit with you for a moment.

If not for the technology in your classroom, what is one experience your students would never be able to have?

When has technology felt like a doorway instead of a distraction? What made the difference?

What is one small way technology could help students see, think, or connect in a way they couldn't without it?

18 **HOLDING MY THINKING**

In the fall of 1993, I sat in my very first math department meeting as a brand-new teacher at North Kansas City High School.

The veteran teachers, whom I loved deeply, were furious. Not annoyed. Not skeptical. Furious.

About calculators.

Graphing calculators, to be precise.

The fear sounded familiar:

"Students won't know how to think."
"They won't learn math."
"They'll just push buttons."

Looking back now, it's almost funny.

Because those same tools eventually opened
doors that had previously been closed to students. They could visualize functions with improved clarity, test ideas, explore patterns, and formulate deeper questions about mathematics.

The calculator didn't replace thinking. It changed how thinking happened.

Thirty years later, the same conversation is happening again – only this time the tool is artificial intelligence.

At first the reaction feels similar: fear that students will stop thinking and start outsourcing their work.

But my own experience with AI made me pause.

I was working on a proof in a graduate-level real analysis course and got stuck. I could follow the mathematics, but I couldn't quite see how to begin.

Instead of asking for the solution, I tried something different.

I asked ChatGPT to explain the problem in two ways: first for a high school senior familiar with only geometric proofs, and then for a third-year undergraduate math major.

The shift was subtle but important.

I wasn't copying an answer.

I was using the explanation to think my way into the problem.

I started asking for hints, starting points, and ways to hold the problem in place while I worked through it.

That's when something clicked.

This wasn't replacing my thinking. It was holding my thinking – a thought partner.

I noticed the same thing when I began shaping the book you're reading now. Over several years, I wrote more than seventy blog posts and grouped twenty-five of them into chapters.

But they didn't read like a book.

Some chapters sounded like a memoir. Others sounded like professional development. A few sounded like workshop outlines.

Total whiplash – no consistency.

So I asked ChatGPT a simple question:

Which voice feels most authentic if this book invites reflection rather than gives answers?

It didn't write the book, but it helped me notice where I sounded like a workshop facilitator instead of a human sharing his thinking while not directing readers to foregone conclusions.

Over dozens of hours, red pen in hand, I revised the manuscript – not because AI wrote it, but because AI helped me see it differently.

Students are already using AI. The real question isn't whether they will use it. It's how.

"Write me 500 words on the Industrial Revolution" isn't thinking.

It's outsourcing.

But imagine students using AI as a thought partner instead:

"Help me clarify my claim."
"Push back on my reasoning."
"What questions am I not considering?"

"Where might my argument be weak?"

When I was in school, my thought partner was a teacher's red pen –
after I finished the work.

What if students had a thought partner during the work?

The writing might be richer. The thinking more complex. The
ownership still theirs.

Maybe this moment isn't really about AI.

Maybe it's another version of the calculator debate.

A new tool.
An old fear.

But if we frame AI as a thought partner – not a shortcut, not a
replacement, not a cheat – it might become what good tools have
always helped us do:

Think more deeply about the world,
about our work,
and about ourselves.

And honestly?

That feels like a worthy endeavor.

If not for AI, I would have never been able to _________________.

Pause and Reflect

Pause for a moment with the question that grew out of this chapter.

Essential Question
What about artificial intelligence?

You don't need to answer this right away. Just notice what happens when you let the question sit with you for a moment.

When you feel genuinely stuck in your thinking, writing, or leadership, who – or what – do you usually turn to?

Where in your work do you value independence so highly that it might unintentionally limit reflection or deeper thinking?

If thinking has always been relational, what possibilities does that open for learning in a world where students no longer think alone?

19 **THE GRAY SPACES**

What goes on in your mind when designing a lesson?

This might be my favorite question to ask a group of teachers – but only when the room is ready for it. Not because it's a clever question, but because it's a dangerous one.

If you ask it too soon, you'll get the safe answers. The ones we've learned to give. The ones that sound like professional development language or interview answers. Nobody lies exactly – but people rarely tell the whole truth either.

When the room feels right, though, something else happens.

A teacher once sat quietly for a while and then answered,
"I'm mostly just trying not to bore my students. Or myself."

The room chuckled with approval.

After a pause, he added,
"I think I'm really chasing emotional impact – for them, and for me."

Beautiful. Not because it was poetic, but because it was honest.

Another teacher said,
"I'm trying to build community. I want ideas to move from
individual students, to small groups, to the whole class and back
again. I don't always know where it's going, but I know there are
certain landmarks I'm hoping we'll pass along the way."

And another:
"I'm always trying to model curiosity. Sometimes that turns into
inquiry. Sometimes it falls flat. Then I adjust."

Those answers don't fit neatly into a lesson plan template.

But they feel like real classrooms.

As a coach of instruction, I often get asked to enforce the current
district or school approved lesson design model. I try to help
teachers find value in those frameworks, but I've never stopped
believing that the real work happens in the gray spaces between
them.

That's where students live.

That's where teachers struggle.

That's where beauty sneaks in.

One teacher told me not long ago,
"After Covid, my students changed. So I had to change too."

Another said,
"My students hate reading. All of it. I don't know what to do yet –
but I'm not giving up."

Two veteran teachers once admitted to each other, for the first time, that they were no longer sure they were still good at this job. Neither of them knew the other felt the same until we explored the winding trail of lesson design.

That moment was uncomfortable.

And healing.

And exactly what teaching really looks like.

Here's what I've learned:

We need anchors. Research matters. Best practices matter. They keep us from drifting too far.

But we also need a compass.

Because classrooms are not oceans we cross in straight lines. They are stormy, human, unpredictable places. And sometimes you don't need another map – you need permission to say,

"I don't know, but I'm still here."

For myself.

And for my students.

So if you lead teachers, coach them, or work alongside them, here's the invitation:

How often do people get to talk honestly about what it feels like to design lessons?

Not only what they're supposed to do – but what they worry about, hope for, and wrestle with?

The fastest path I've ever found into those conversations isn't a new framework.

It's good questions.

Asked inside trusting relationships.

When that happens, the masks come off.

And learning – real learning – starts again.

Pause and Reflect

Pause for a moment with the question that grew out of this chapter.

Essential Question

What goes on in your mind when designing a lesson?

You don't need to answer this right away. Just notice what happens when you let the question sit with you for a moment.

When you sit down to plan a lesson, what is the first thing you usually think about – content, time, behavior, or how students might experience it?

Which parts of lesson design feel solid and safe for you – and which parts feel uncertain, emotional, or risky?

If you could tell the truth without being judged, what do you most hope students feel when they walk into your classroom tomorrow?

WHEN LEARNING BEGINS TO SPEAK

I've shared a handful of ways I've tried to think about lessons – not as scripts to follow, but as invitations into thinking. None of these are formulas. They're simply ways of paying closer attention to what's happening while learning is still alive.

Because that's what instruction is, at its best:

How we create conditions where thinking can surface, collide, a nd grow.

The questions in this part all circle the same quiet idea:

How will I design learning so I can see, hear, and respond to what my students are actually doing with it?

There isn't one right design.

But there are always consequences – for understanding, for confusion, and for whether students feel like their thinking matters.

When we design for activity, we get busy rooms.

When we design for thinking, we get learning.

And the difference is rarely dramatic.

It shows up in where we pause.

In what we listen for.

In whether we let ideas breathe before we move on.

Which brings us naturally to what comes next.

Once you decide how you want to be with students,
and how you want learning to unfold,
the next question becomes unavoidable:

How will you know if it's working?

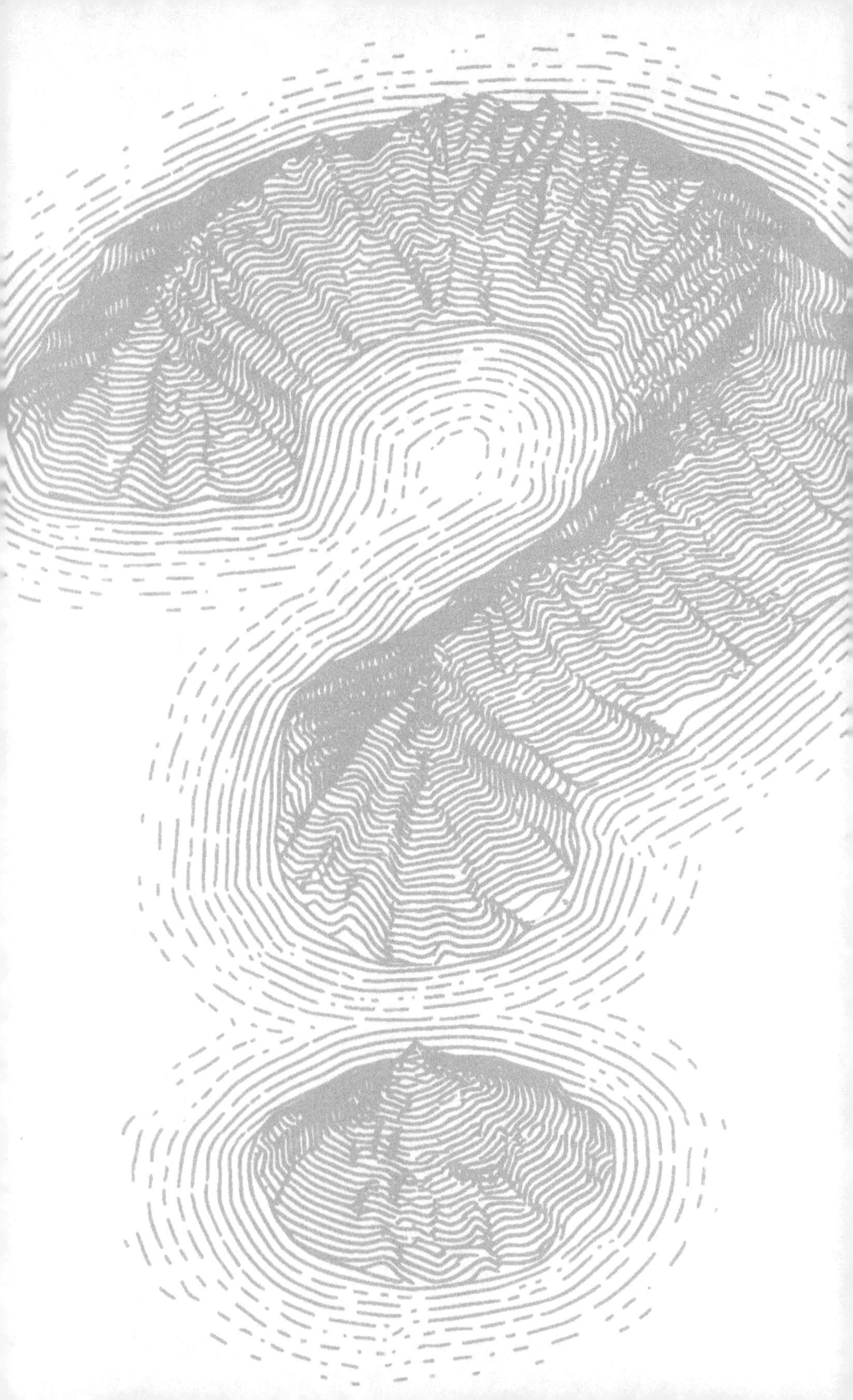

PART 4

BECOMING

A SOCIETY GROWS GREAT WHEN OLD MEN PLANT TREES WHOSE SHADE THEY KNOW THEY SHALL NEVER SIT IN.
GREEK PROVERB

ON BECOMING

The freedom to choose who you will be.

Until now, the questions in this book have primarily existed within the classroom.

They've asked how we behave with students.
How relationships shape the conditions for learning.
How can educators design lessons to allow thinking to surface?

Those questions all matter.

But if you stay in this work long enough, another question begins to appear – one that is quieter, and harder to answer.

Not about your lessons.
Not about your strategies.
About you.

Who am I becoming as a teacher?

Because over time, teaching stops being something you simply do, and becomes part of who you are.

The next chapters focus on identity, not just techniques. They explore the small choices, habits, and perspectives that shape who you become as a teacher over the years.

20 **REAL CHANGE DOESN'T CLICK**

Some questions shape a single lesson. Others shape the rest of
your career.
One question did that for me.

I wish I could tell you that it clicks on a Tuesday. Or after the third
try. Or right after the training ends.

But that's not how it works.

When I look back at my first five years in the classroom, I honestly
believed my students were engaged. They were quiet. They were
looking at me. They were doing the work. I took that as proof.

It wasn't.

Eye contact isn't thinking. Neat desks in rows aren't learning.
You can borrow enthusiasm for a while.

What I didn't know yet was that real engagement has a sound –
and I hadn't learned how to hear it. It has a messiness to it. Students
arguing, wondering, trying things that don't quite work yet.

And I didn't know how to listen for that –
or how to create the conditions for it.

So I started stepping into unfamiliar territory. Sometimes it came from a mentor. Sometimes from an evaluator. Sometimes from a comment that annoyed me more than it should have.

I remember a post-observation conversation in the late '90s in a small office off the main hallway that left me completely unconvinced. I smiled, nodded, and walked out thinking:

Does this person even know what it's like to stand in front of a room full of teenagers?

The administrator told me to write every student question asked in class on the right-hand side of my limited board space. And then review each question at the end of each class to ensure that I have given answers. It sounded ridiculous to me.

And yet later that day, a little voice kept whispering in my ear.

They did notice something.

Almost no one asked questions.

What if that matters?

I didn't change everything. But I went looking. I talked to a mentor, signed up for a conference, and tried two small shifts – I started modeling questions. And then I started teaching students how to ask their own.

That's how it usually starts.

Not with certainty but with curiosity.

At the time, I was experimenting. I didn't realize I was learning how to recognize real engagement.

Years later, I saw curiosity unfolding in a pair co-teachers in their "lower level" Algebra 1 classrooms. Their students struggled. Some had learning disabilities. Some didn't believe they were "math people."

And those teachers decided to adopt a different teaching approach. They asked students to wrestle with problems before asking for help. To figure out what to do when they weren't sure what to do.

The first year was rough. The teachers questioned themselves constantly.

Students had to think more, but they often felt frustrated or bored. They rarely found the right flow in problem-solving and exploration. The teachers were struggling with both the mechanics of such a classroom approach and the nuance needed to be flexible and confident.

The second year, something started to settle.

When I walked into their classroom, I didn't look at the teachers.

I looked at the kids.

They were on their feet. They were at whiteboards. They were arguing about math in full sentences. They were using the language of the subject. They were trying, failing, trying again.

By October in year two, this was normal. It was their classroom culture.

By the third year, the two teachers with struggling students – those everyone worried about – outperformed not only similar classes but also many regular and advanced students on the state exam.

But honestly, that wasn't the part that gave me chills.

It was the sound and movement of student thinking.

No test prep. No worksheets grinding away. Just kids wrestling with ideas together.

Three years of awkward lessons. Three years of adjusting. Three years of "Are we sure this is working?"

And then one day, it was.

Not because the teachers got better at controlling the room – but because they got better at trusting the unpredictable, often messy process.

That's what I wish someone had told me when I was 25 and panicking about whether I was any good at this.

Because the question that haunted me back then was simple:

When will it click?

Real change doesn't click.

It grows.
It stumbles.
It argues.
It gains strength as you continue to doubt it.

So if you're trying something new right now and it feels clumsy and slow –

good.

You're in the middle of it.

Don't give up.

That's where all the best teaching lives.

Pause and Reflect

Pause for a moment with the question that grew out of this chapter.

Essential Question
I am trying something new in class… when will it click?

You don't need to answer this right away. Just notice what happens when you let the question sit with you for a moment.

What's something you're trying right now that feels awkward, slow, or unfinished – and what would it mean to stay with it a little longer?

When you think about your students, where do you see signs of real thinking beginning to surface, even if the results aren't there yet?

If growth in your classroom takes years, not weeks, how might that change what you expect from yourself this semester?

21 A QUESTION THAT WON'T LEAVE YOU ALONE

When a question really gets its hooks into you, it tends to disturb things. It unsettles your routines. It pokes at habits you didn't realize you had – or it opens you up to new possibilities.

That's a good sign.

But it's also the moment when a lot of good ideas quietly die – not because they were wrong, but because they were uncomfortable.

Over the years, I started to notice a pattern in how meaningful change took root – for me and for the teachers I worked with.

It usually began with curiosity.

Sometimes that came from research. Sometimes it came from a conversation in the copy room. Sometimes it came from watching a colleague do something and thinking,

Wait – why did that work so well?

However it arrives, that first phase is about gathering ideas, stories, evidence, and possibilities.

Not solutions.

Just a wider field of view.

Then came the scary part.

At some point you stop reading and thinking, and start doing.

You try the thing. You shift a routine. You ask a different kind of question in class. You design a lesson in a new way.

One semester, I decided to experiment with how students explained their thinking. Instead of asking for answers, I asked groups to show their reasoning on the board and talk through it with the class.

The first day felt awkward.

Some students froze. A few tried to dominate the conversation. Others looked at me as if to say, Are you really going to make us do this?

But by the next week something interesting happened.

Students started listening to each other.

They began building on one another's ideas instead of waiting for mine.

It wasn't perfect.

But it was different.

And that difference made me curious enough to keep going.

This is where risk shows up – not the dramatic kind, but the quiet professional kind. You're standing in front of students trying something that might flop, knowing that the outcome isn't guaranteed.

After that, if you're honest, comes reflection.

Not just How did I feel about it?

But:

What just happened?

Did students engage differently?

Did their thinking surface?

Did the learning move?

Sometimes the answer is yes.

Sometimes it's no.

Often it's – sort of.

But reflection is where the story starts to become clearer.

And once you can see the story, you get to refine it. You keep what worked. You let go of what didn't. You adjust. You tweak. You make the next version just a little better than the last one.

Then you do it again.

Not because you're chasing perfection, but because this is growth. It's a series of imperfect tries based on what you learned last time.

Over time, I started naming that rhythm for myself – not as a checklist, but as a way to keep moving when things felt messy. I called it the five Rs:

Research → Risk → Reflect → Refine → Repeat

Not once.

Not in a straight line.

But over and over, in small loops.

That cycle is the difference between a courageous and compelling thirty-year career and a single year repeated thirty times.

The teachers who keep learning don't avoid risk.

They get better at walking back through it with curiosity instead of disappointment.

And it all starts with a question that refuses to let you stay the same.

A question you discover is essential to you.

Pause and Reflect

Pause for a moment with the question that grew out of this chapter.

Essential Question
I am working through a compelling essential question… any advice?

You don't need to answer this right away. Just notice what happens when you let the question sit with you for a moment.

What question has been quietly bothering you in your teaching lately – the one you keep circling back to even when you try to ignore it?

Where are you right now in the cycle of Research → Risk → Reflect → Refine → Repeat – and what might the next small step look like?

What would it mean to treat your next instructional experiment as part of a longer story, not a one-shot success or failure?

22 WHEN TEACHING BECOMES YOURS

For a long time, I believed that teaching primarily involved improving my ability to follow what was labeled as "best practice." Better strategies. Better frameworks. Better pacing. Better management. And all of that mattered.

It still does.

But at some point, I realized something else was happening beneath the surface. I wasn't just learning how to teach. I was gradually uncovering the extent of my actual freedom.

Not freedom in the sense of doing whatever I wanted.

But freedom in the deeper sense of choosing how I wanted to show up – with students, with colleagues, and with myself.

Freedom didn't arrive as a lightning bolt. It appeared as a series of small, uncomfortable moments: trying something new in class, watching it fall flat, reflecting, and trying again. Sometimes there was research behind it. Sometimes there was a colleague beside me. I often found myself alone in my classroom after the bell, contemplating what I would change for tomorrow – or the next class in five minutes.

Each time I went through that cycle of experimenting and reflecting,

I stepped away from simply copying "how teaching is done" and moved toward something more personal.

More honest.

More mine.

That's where freedom started to live. Not in rejecting research or ignoring expertise, but in deciding what I would do with what I had learned.

That's also why essential questions have always meant so much to me. A good essential question doesn't tell you what to think. It creates a space where you have to decide.

That space – between what others have told you and what you choose to do – is where freedom lives.

Over the years I've also learned something else.

People don't usually need to be fixed.

They need to be heard.

When a teacher feels frustrated, tired, or unsure, the most powerful thing I can often do isn't give advice. It's to listen – without interrupting, without redirecting, without jumping to solutions.

Just listening.

And as the story unfolds, something interesting happens. People start to hear themselves think. They notice their own contradictions. They discover their own longings. And sometimes, without any advice at all, a new possibility appears.

That's freedom too.

Not someone handing you a solution –

but you realizing you already have choices.

Yes, sometimes we do bring in experience, perspective, or a story of our own. But only after the person has had space to understand what they are actually wrestling with.

Freedom grows in that kind of room.

There are experts everywhere – best practices, frameworks, and gurus as far as the eye can see. But after you listen to all that, one question always remains:

What will you choose to do?

That answer – whether spoken or not – becomes your path.

And that's when teaching becomes not just effective.

But yours.

Pause and Reflect

Pause for a moment with the question that grew out of this chapter.

Essential Question
Where is your freedom in your teaching?

You don't need to answer this right away. Just notice what happens when you let the question sit with you for a moment.

When was the last time you made a choice in your teaching that felt truly yours – not borrowed from a book, a coach, or a mandate? What did that feel like?

Where do you notice yourself following "how it's supposed to be done" when something inside you wants to try something different?

If you gave yourself a little more permission to listen – to students, to colleagues, or to your own instincts – what might change about the way you show up tomorrow?

23 CHOOSING MEANING

There are few moments in education that are more predictable than this one.

You walk into a big room – tables, coffee, a screen at the front, someone like me about to start talking. You might feel excited. You might be tired. You might already be secretly calculating how long until lunch.

From the front of the room, I can usually see all of it.

I've learned something important over the years: professional learning doesn't just happen to us. It happens within us – or not at all.

Most of us learned a long time ago how to sit politely, take a few notes, and wait it out. We learned how to be compliant.

What we didn't always learn was how to stay alive in those rooms.

That realization started to change for me because of Peter Block.

Years ago, in one of his trainings, he didn't begin with content or a framework. Instead, he put four questions on the screen and then stepped aside.

The room went quiet. People shifted in their chairs. Phones came out to photograph the slide.

Something inside the room started to move.

Not because the questions were clever – but because they were personal.

They didn't ask, "What do you hope to learn today?"

They asked something much more personal:

Who are you going to be while you're here?

Over time, those questions became my favorite way to kick off any learning experience. It doesn't matter if I'm leading or I'm the learner sitting in the room.

They go something like this:

How much do I intend to get value from this?
How willing am I to engage?
How open am I to taking a risk?
What is my responsibility for the learning of others in this room?

That's it.

No strategies. No jargon.

Just a quiet invitation to stop being a passive passenger.

Every time I use these questions, I watch something shift.

Last spring I was leading a session on classroom discussion strategies. About halfway through, I asked the first question:

How much do I intend to get value from this?

A teacher in the third row lowered her notebook and said in a soft voice, "I guess I haven't really thought about that before."

A few people nearby nodded.

The room didn't transform instantly, but something loosened. A few minutes later, it was time for a small-group activity. That same teacher volunteered to go first. She had clearly been avoiding this earlier.

Others followed.

The conversation that emerged wasn't perfect, but it was real. Teachers started building on each other's ideas instead of waiting for mine.

It was subtle.

But the energy in the room had shifted.

Not because the training suddenly became magical –

but because people had decided to show up differently.

That's the part we don't talk about enough.

You don't have control over who's presenting. You don't have control over the agenda.

But you almost always have some control over how you enter the room.

You can walk in guarded.

You can walk in cynical.
You can walk in tired.

Or you can walk in curious.

You can decide, quietly:

I'm going to look for something here.
I'm going to bring something with me.
I'm going to be part of this, not just sit through it.

That choice doesn't make everything wonderful, but it can make it meaningful.

And meaning is the one thing no one else can give you.

You must choose it.

Pause and Reflect

Pause for a moment with the question that grew out of this chapter.

Essential Question
What is my role in this room?

You don't need to answer this right away. Just notice what happens when you let the question sit with you for a moment.

When you walk into professional learning, do you tend to arrive as a passenger or a participant? What usually decides that for you?

What would it look like for you to take just a little more responsibility for the energy and learning in the room the next time you attend a session?

If you treated your next professional learning experience as a chance to contribute – not just consume – what might you do differently?

24 **UNFINISHED**

I've been thinking a lot about age lately. Not in the "how did I get this old?" way – though that sneaks in too – but in the quieter, more curious way. The kind that wonders whether we're actually growing up… or growing into who we were always meant to be.

I realized recently that, in a strange and very mathematical way, I'm living my fourth version of being eighteen.

Not in energy or knees or metabolism – clearly not. But in something deeper: curiosity, choice, responsibility, effort, identity.

If we're lucky, we get more than one eighteen in a lifetime.

The first one is the obvious one: childhood through young adulthood.

School is compulsory, but effort isn't. You have to show up, but you don't have to care. And the truth is, almost no one fully understands how much that combination – mandatory attendance and optional effort – can influence everything that comes later.

We all hear the warnings.

"This matters."
"It opens doors."
"You'll thank yourself later."

But it's hard to feel the weight of doors you haven't yet seen or don't know exist.

If I could go back and whisper something to my eighteen-year-old self, it wouldn't be about grades or transcripts. It would be this:

Every choice you make opens some doors and quietly closes others. You won't know which ones matter most until much later. All you can do now is invest in keeping as many doors open as you can.

Then comes the second eighteen – the one that sneaks up on you while you're learning how much milk costs and how fast paychecks disappear.

Education is no longer compulsory, but life still is.

Work. Bills. Relationships. Fatigue.

You start realizing time and effort are no longer abstract.

They're limited resources.

This is where learning becomes a choice again, but now it competes with everything else.

This is where some people keep growing.

And some people quietly stop.

I don't have tidy advice for this stage, because it's messy by nature. But I know this: when you keep choosing to learn – about your body, your mind, your work, your relationships – you keep expanding who you're becoming.

When you stop, things don't stay still.

They shrink.

The third eighteen is where the illusion creeps in. The feeling that you know enough. That you've seen enough. That maybe this is just who you are now.

That's the dangerous part – not aging, but arriving.

This is where I've had to learn that nobody is coming to save me from my own stagnation. If I want to keep growing, I have to keep choosing discomfort.

New ideas.
New skills.
New questions.

Not because I'm broken – but because I'm unfinished.

And now here I am, creeping into what I'll call the fourth eighteen.

A place where learning and effort are no longer automatic. They have to be chosen – again, on purpose, every day.

I try to imagine what a seventy-two-year-old version of me would say to the fifty-six-year-old version sitting here typing now.

I don't hear a list of accomplishments. I hear reminders.

Be present with people.
Move your body.

Feed your mind with things that stretch it.
Sit quietly sometimes and listen to what your heart is pointing
toward – even if it isn't giving you a map.

Keep learning.
Keep loving.
Keep noticing.

Not because you have to.

Because you get to.

Which brings me back to the question.

Are we growing up – or growing into?

The best lives do both. But the second one – the growing into – only
happens if we keep choosing effort, curiosity, and learning long
after no one is making us.

That's how I've come to understand education.

Not as something that ends with a diploma, or even a career –

but as the way we keep becoming.

And I hope – for all of us –

that we never finish.

Pause and Reflect

Pause for a moment with the question that grew out of this chapter.

Essential Question
Are we growing up or into?

You don't need to answer this right away. Just notice what happens when you let the question sit with you for a moment.

Which "eighteen" do you feel like you're in right now – and what might that say about what you're learning, choosing, or avoiding?

Where have you noticed yourself starting to believe "I already know enough"? What might be waiting just beyond that belief?

If a future version of you were sitting beside you right now, what do you think they would gently encourage you to keep leaning into?

25 THE HEROIC JOURNEY

Your teaching life is usually pretty steady.

The faces change from class to class and year to year, but you – and the content – mostly stay the same. You build a style, a way of being, a rhythm. You learn how to work with a variety of students, colleagues, administrators, and yes, parents. Over time, you figure out what works for you and you settle into it.

And then something nudges you – not dramatically, not all at once, just enough to make you look up.

The Call to Adventure (or a Conference)

It doesn't have to be a conference. It might be a professional development day, a staff meeting, or a hallway conversation. But you're called – or voluntold – to be somewhere at a certain time.

You take your seat. You half-listen, scroll, doodle, wait.

And then someone says something that makes you pause.

You lean toward the person on your left.
"Wait… what did the presenter just say?"

"I think something about enhancing lectures."

You nudge the person on your right.
"Did you catch that?"

"Yeah – something about how we tell too much and don't create enough conditions for students to think. Page seven."

You flip to page seven.

And suddenly it hits you.

This is actually good.

Your mind starts racing. You see tomorrow's lesson in a new way. You can't wait to try it.

Failure

It didn't work.

The next day you tried the strategy and it fell flat – the kids were confused, you were confused, and it felt awkward and clunky, nothing like the smooth version you imagined in your head.

Maybe this isn't for me, you think.

Later that week you run into your table partners from the training.

"Hey – I tried that thing from the conference."

"Oh yeah? How did it go?"

"Honestly? Not great. It was a mess."

They laugh.

One says, "That's exactly what happened to me – until I figured
something out…"

The Mentor

Next to a jammed copier and a pile of half-printed worksheets, they
share their stories – what they tried, what went wrong, what they
changed, and what finally worked.

They aren't experts or gurus – just teachers a few steps ahead on the
same road.

Before they walk away, one of them turns and says,
"Try it again. Just… different this time."

And you do.

Crossing the Threshold

You take risks, reflect, refine, repeat.

The strategy begins to change – not into something from the
training handout, but into something that fits you and your students.
Your lessons start to feel different. Lighter. More alive.

Your students are the ones who benefit.

Every so often, you and your copy-room mentors check in. You
share wins. You share frustrations. You learn.

And then there's that one class.

The one where nothing seems to work the way it does
everywhere else.

The Inner Cave

At a department meeting your leader asks,
"Anyone have something to share?"

Before you can stop yourself, your hand floats upward.

You feel all the eyes on you before you see them.

You talk about the training – the risks, the mess, the slow progress,
the students.

You're not sure anyone is really listening.

But a few heads nod.

Afterward, someone stops you.
"Hey – can you tell me more about what you tried?"

And suddenly you realize something.

Your story matters.

The Final Boss

That difficult class is still difficult.

And one day it clicks – not in a triumphant way, but in a
curious one.

These techniques, the way you've been using them, aren't right for
this group.

And instead of feeling defeated, you feel interested.

What else might work here?

A new door appears.

The Road Back

At the next department meeting, you share again – not just the successes, but the questions, the adjustments, and the humility that came with them.

This time the room feels different.

People are really listening.

Afterward, another colleague pulls you aside.
"I've been thinking about what you said…"

And just like that, your journey continues.

Future You

Years pass faster than you expect.

One afternoon you find yourself in your half-packed classroom – posters coming down, desk drawers emptied, a career being quietly folded into cardboard boxes. The desks are slightly out of order, a few still crooked from the last class.

You sit down in one of them.

The room feels different without students in it.

Quieter.
Lighter.
Like it's holding its breath.

A colleague – maybe an assistant principal you've worked with for years – lingers in the doorway.

They step inside.
Pull a chair close.
Look around.
Then at you.

"So," they ask softly,
"what was it all about?"

You don't rush to answer.

You think about the risks – the failed lessons, the difficult class that made you curious instead of defeated.

The copy-room conversations. The colleagues who leaned in.

And the students, over the years.

You think about the moments that didn't look heroic at all.

And you smile.

"I wanted them to learn," you say.
"And I wanted them to think for themselves."

You pause.

"And somewhere along the way…

I did too."

And the questions keep coming.

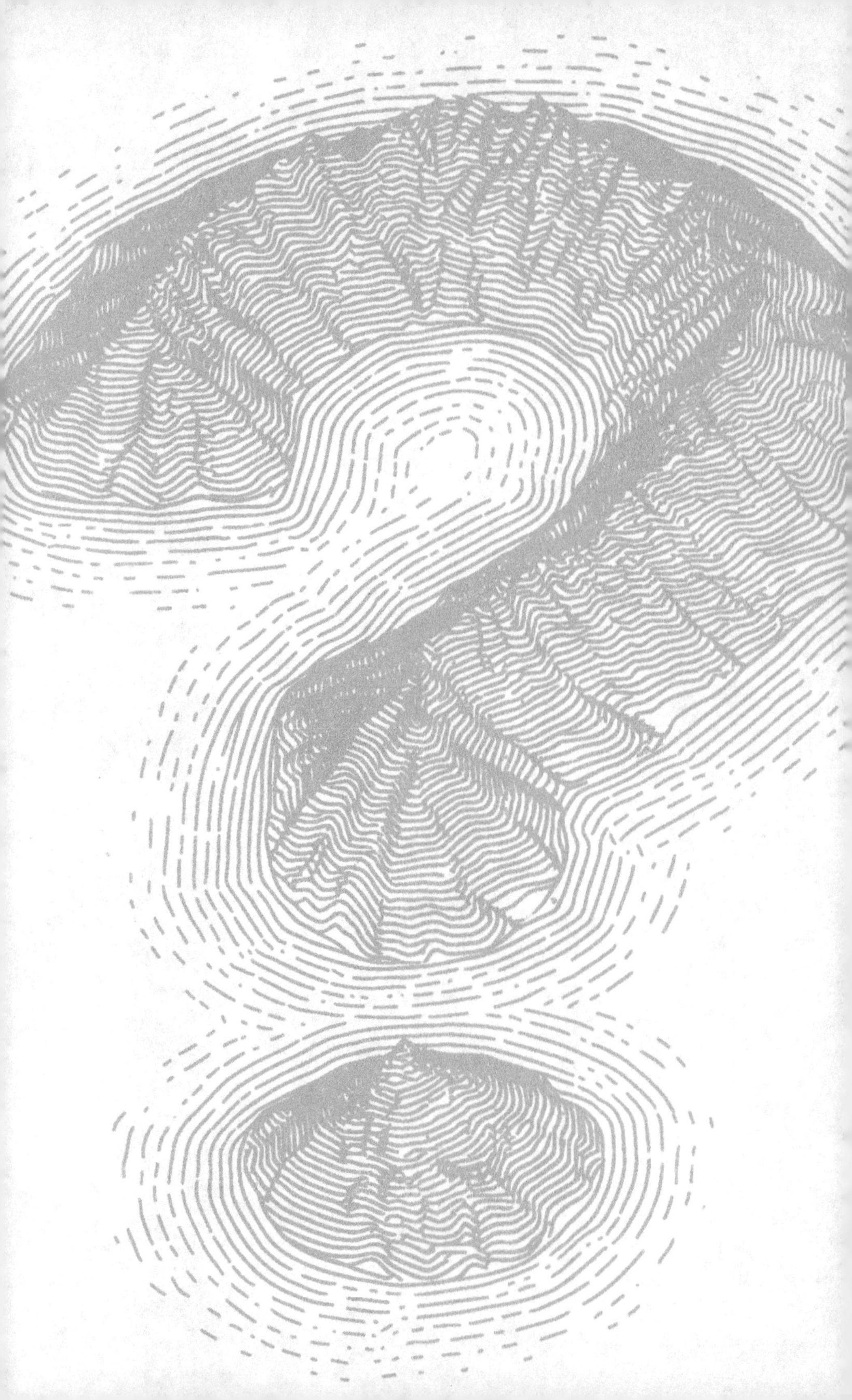

ACKNOWLEDGEMENTS

Over more than three decades in education, many people have shaped how I think about teaching, leadership, and learning. I can't name them all here, but a few deserve special mention.

There are mentors who may not know the role they've played in my life, but I feel compelled to name them: William Sommers, Robert Garmston, Art Costa, Jennifer Abrams, Peter Block, and Edgar Schein. And MK Mueller, who looked me in the eyes in 2014 and asked, "What would you do if you had no fear?"

Truman High School in Independence, Missouri, in the early 2000s was a special place. I don't know what it was before or after, but I know what it was then. Kristel Barr, our principal, modeled the kind of leadership that stays with you. For over seven years we met weekly – reflecting on the past, planning for the future, and occasionally offering local restaurant recommendations. Alongside district mentors like Henry Russell, Ed Streich, and Cliff Mohn, she helped create something rare: a place where teachers and leaders felt trusted, challenged, and supported.

I was also fortunate to work with teacher leaders such as Chris Adams, Ann Hay, Christina Hocker, Jean Luzader, Jeff Roudebush, and Karen Smith during that time. I learned from them daily.

Larry Gregg, my graduate professor at the University of Missouri–Kansas City, still shows up in my thinking. He introduced me to constructivism and mental models – not as theories, but as ways of seeing. Those ideas changed how I lead, coach, and live.

At the American Alliance for Innovative Systems, I found a professional home. David Holden – our late CEO and my dear friend – was one of the smartest and kindest people I've known. AAIS cofounder, Robin Shrode, took a chance on me in 2008, and I'm grateful she did. And I'm grateful for every colleague at AAIS, past and present, who keeps pushing me to think more deeply about education.

Hayet Woods, Venita Thurman, Lisa Thomas, Joe Hessman, Drew Smith, and Glenna Bult taught me more about leadership than any book could. I know I provided a wide spectrum of growth opportunities (what to do – and what not to do) for them along the way as well.

Eric Creeger – thank you for that hotel lobby conversation in 2022. When you told me to stop talking about writing a book and begin writing a blog, something shifted within me.

Finally, my family. They let me disappear into this project without ever making me feel guilty for it. For that, and for them, I am deeply grateful.

ABOUT THE AUTHOR

Bill Brooks has spent more than thirty years in education as a classroom teacher, school leader, instructional coach, and national consultant. He began his career in 1992 as a middle and high school math teacher and later taught at the college level before moving into instructional support and school leadership.

Over the course of his career, Bill has worked closely with educators to improve instruction, build professional learning communities, and create classroom conditions that make student thinking visible and meaningful. His work has included roles as an assistant principal, instructional coach, and Secondary Schools Redesign Coordinator focused on improving teaching and learning in large, comprehensive schools.

Today, Bill works nationally with schools, districts, and educational organizations through the American Alliance for Innovative Systems (AAIS). He supports teachers, instructional coaches, and school leaders in curriculum, instruction, assessment, and professional learning design, often modeling classroom instruction across grades K–12 in multiple subject areas. As of 2025, he has completed more than 500 days of on-site consulting work in schools across the United States.

Bill is also the creator and host of the EQ4E (Essential Questions for Educators) podcast and author of the Essential Questions for Educators blog at essentialquestionsforeducators.com.

This book grows directly out of his work alongside thousands of educators in classrooms, coaching conversations, and professional learning communities.